Linking art to the world around us

Arty Facts

Animals
& Art Activities

W9-ART-695

Crabtree Publishing Company
www.crabtreebooks.com

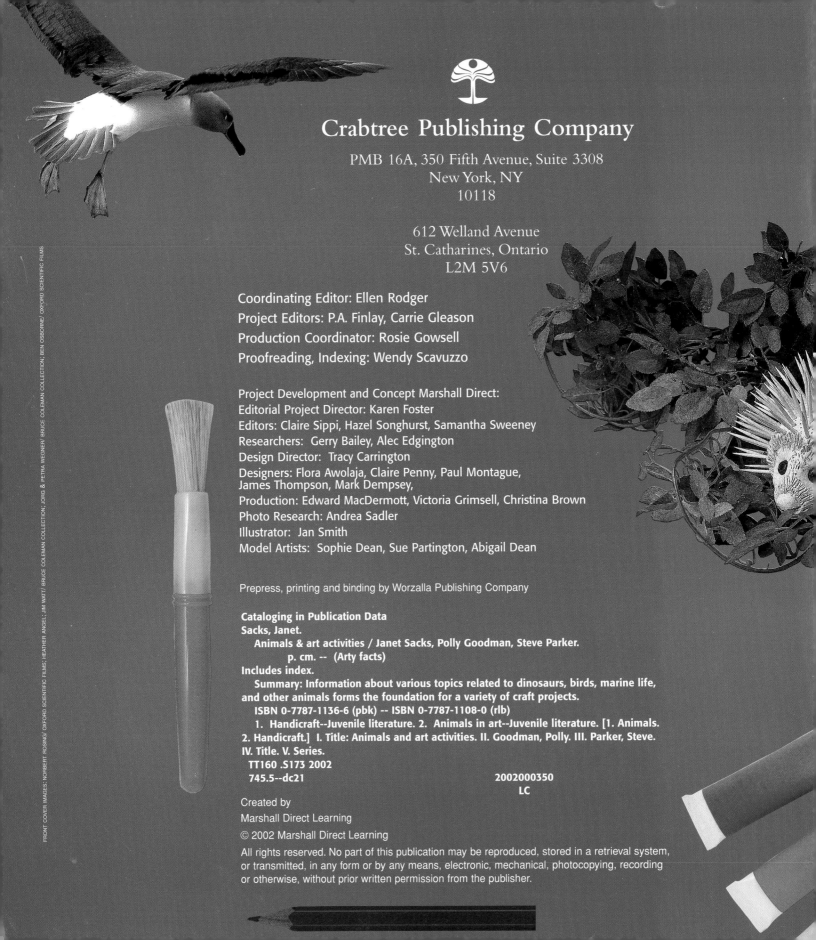

Crabtree Publishing Company

PMB 16A, 350 Fifth Avenue, Suite 3308
New York, NY
10118

612 Welland Avenue
St. Catharines, Ontario
L2M 5V6

Coordinating Editor: Ellen Rodger
Project Editors: P.A. Finlay, Carrie Gleason
Production Coordinator: Rosie Gowsell
Proofreading, Indexing: Wendy Scavuzzo

Project Development and Concept Marshall Direct:
Editorial Project Director: Karen Foster
Editors: Claire Sippi, Hazel Songhurst, Samantha Sweeney
Researchers: Gerry Bailey, Alec Edgington
Design Director: Tracy Carrington
Designers: Flora Awolaja, Claire Penny, Paul Montague,
James Thompson, Mark Dempsey,
Production: Edward MacDermott, Victoria Grimsell, Christina Brown
Photo Research: Andrea Sadler
Illustrator: Jan Smith
Model Artists: Sophie Dean, Sue Partington, Abigail Dean

Prepress, printing and binding by Worzalla Publishing Company

Cataloging in Publication Data
Sacks, Janet.
   Animals & art activities / Janet Sacks, Polly Goodman, Steve Parker.
         p. cm. -- (Arty facts)
Includes index.
   **Summary: Information about various topics related to dinosaurs, birds, marine life,
and other animals forms the foundation for a variety of craft projects.**
   ISBN 0-7787-1136-6 (pbk) -- ISBN 0-7787-1108-0 (rlb)
   **1. Handicraft--Juvenile literature. 2. Animals in art--Juvenile literature. [1. Animals.
2. Handicraft.] I. Title: Animals and art activities. II. Goodman, Polly. III. Parker, Steve.
IV. Title. V. Series.**
   TT160 .S173 2002
   745.5--dc21   **2002000350**
                                                      LC

Created by
Marshall Direct Learning
© 2002 Marshall Direct Learning

All rights reserved. No part of this publication may be reproduced, stored in a retrieval system,
or transmitted, in any form or by any means, electronic, mechanical, photocopying, recording
or otherwise, without prior written permission from the publisher.

FRONT COVER IMAGES: NORBERT ROSING/ OXFORD SCIENTIFIC FILMS; HEATHER ANGEL, JIM WATT/ BRUCE COLEMAN COLLECTION; JÖRG & PETRA WEGNER/ BRUCE COLEMAN COLLECTION; BEN OSBORNE/ OXFORD SCIENTIFIC FILMS

Linking art to the world around us

Arty Facts

Animals
& Art Activities

Contents

WRITTEN BY Janet Sacks, Polly Goodman, Steve Parker

Dinosaurs

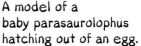
A model of a baby parasaurolophus hatching out of an egg.

Carnivores

Some dinosaurs were gigantic, fearsome hunters with large mouths, massive teeth, and curving claws. The tyrannosaurus rex was 40 feet (12 m) long, with an enormous head. The giganotosaurus was even bigger – as long as 43 feet (13 m), with a mouth the size of a small car. The compsognathus was chicken-sized and darted around hunting small animals.

Giants

The diplodocus and brachiosaurus were herbivores, or plant-eaters. They were nearly twice as long as a transport truck, and more than twice as heavy. The maiasauras guarded their eggs in a nest scooped out of the soil. They brought their **hatchlings** berries, leaves, and plants to eat, and protected them from hungry **predators**.

No survivors

The Age of Dinosaurs spanned from about 230 million to 65 million years ago. Then, suddenly, the dinosaurs all died out. No one really knows why. Many scientists believe that Earth was hit by a giant lump of rock from outer space called an asteroid. The asteroid caused a massive explosion and dust cloud that brought years of cold and darkness, killing all the dinosaurs. Some close relatives of the dinosaurs are living today – birds, and **reptiles**, such as crocodiles.

Millions of years ago, in prehistoric times, giant **dinosaurs** lived on the Earth. They were some of the biggest, fastest, and fiercest animals there has ever been. They lived in all parts of the world, in many different surroundings. They ate every kind of food, and some even ate each other!

Animals

Model dinorama

WHAT YOU NEED

colored Plasticine

poster board

paints and brush

stick

1 Shape your Plasticine to create a collection of dinosaurs.

2 Use the stick to add patterns and texture to the Plasticine.

Make a leafy prehistoric scene to put your dinosaurs in

3 Paint a leafy scene on white poster board to make a backdrop for your dinosaurs.

Showing off!

Many birds in the **rainforests** of South America and on tropical Pacific islands **display** very bright, colorful feathers. Their feathers are a natural work of art, but they have a practical purpose as well. Bright feathers help the male bird to attract a female during the **mating** season.

Birds of paradise

The bird of paradise is one of the most beautiful birds in the world. There are more than 40 different varieties, and most of these live on the tropical island of New Guinea. They live in forests, where they feed on fruits and insects. Before the mating season, the male birds gather in trees to display their brightly colored feathers to the dull-colored females. Their **plumage** grows in many strange forms and colors. Birds of paradise strut and dance and spread out their feathers so that they can be more easily seen.

Greater bird of paradise

The greater bird of paradise is one of the most exotically plumed birds in the world. Its forehead and throat are emerald green, its head is golden yellow, and its wings and tail are maroon. From under its wings sprout dense feathers about two feet (61 cm) long.

Courtship

The males perform a mating dance, or courtship display. After the female has chosen a mate, she builds a nest and lays up to three eggs in it.

A beautiful tropical bird with bright red plumage.

Animals

Color-crazy bird

WHAT YOU NEED

pencil

toilet paper rolls

scissors

egg carton

colored paper

wire

glue

tape

construction paper

tissue paper

1 Cut a small section from the toilet paper roll. Cut a beak shape from the egg carton and wedge it into the smaller roll.

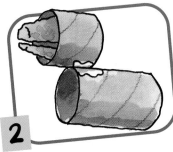

2 Glue the smaller part of the roll on top of the larger section to make the bird's head.

3 Use wire to make two legs with feet. Poke the legs through the base of the body. Bend them so that the bird stands firmly. Tape them in place.

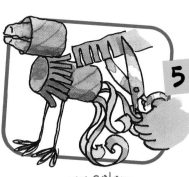

4 Cut strips of colored paper. Twist them around a pencil to make curly tail feathers.

5 Cut more strips to make a fringe and glue this around the body.

How many colors will your bird have?

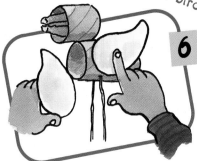

6 Cut two wings out of construction paper and glue them to each side of the bird. Decorate the wings with strips of colored paper.

You can add real feathers too!

7 Scrunch up tissue paper into small balls and cover the throat and head of your bird.

Patches and stripes

The **animal kingdom** is a stunning display of skin patterns and colors. Male peacocks use their dazzling patterns to attract a mate. For zebras, tigers, giraffes, and many other animals, their patterns are more than just a fashion display or an opportunity to show off. They are a matter of life or death.

Hidden hunters

Tigers live in the forests and tall grasslands of Asia. Their orange-and-black stripes let them move almost unseen, while stealthily stalking an antelope or deer. Without its **camouflage** and hunting skills, the tiger would starve. The pattern on each tiger is unique – no other tiger's pattern is exactly the same.

Safe in the shade

A giraffe's coat has a patchy brown pattern. Standing among the trees in the dappled sunlight, giraffes can be surprisingly difficult to see. While feeding, they need to stay as hidden from prowling lions as possible.

Spot the herd

Each zebra's black-and-white striped coat is unique. The different patterns help zebras recognize their own **herd** among the many others that roam the grassy plains. The safest place for zebras to be is in the herd. The more ears listening for an approaching lion, the better the chance the herd has to gallop away.

Animals

WHAT YOU NEED

poster board

tape

black paper

scissors

black paint

brush

bamboo stick

pencil

Zebra mask

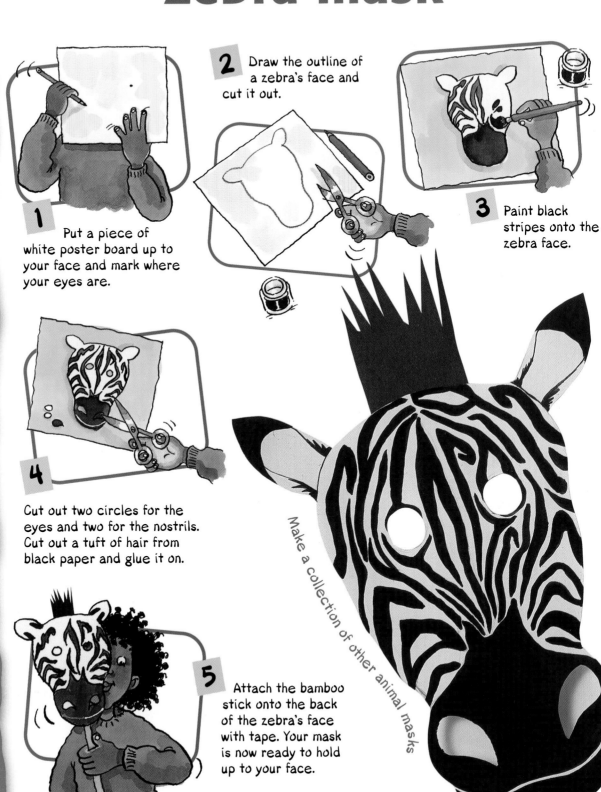

1 Put a piece of white poster board up to your face and mark where your eyes are.

2 Draw the outline of a zebra's face and cut it out.

3 Paint black stripes onto the zebra face.

4 Cut out two circles for the eyes and two for the nostrils. Cut out a tuft of hair from black paper and glue it on.

5 Attach the bamboo stick onto the back of the zebra's face with tape. Your mask is now ready to hold up to your face.

Make a collection of other animal masks

9

Super scales

Fish and reptiles, such as snakes and lizards, are covered with flat plates called scales. These small, hard scales protect the animal's soft body. Turtles and crocodiles have large, bony, armor-like plates instead of scales. The pangolin is the only **mammal** with scales. It looks like a big pine cone with legs!

Sharp or smooth

Some fish have thin, bony scales with rounded edges, but the way the scales lie on their bodies actually makes them smooth to touch. Other fish have scales with tiny, sharp points on the surface, so they feel rough. A shark's skin looks very smooth, but is covered with overlapping scales that look like tiny teeth.

Most predators cannot break through the scaly skin of a pangolin.

Second skin

Snakes have dry, overlapping scales. They even have clear scales over their eyes. Several times a year, a new scaly skin grows under the old one. The snake wiggles out of its worn skin head-first, rubbing itself against rocks to help get the old skin off.

Body armor

A turtle's shell has two layers of bony plates. The inner layer is part of the **skeleton**. Horny, joined plates called **scutes** make up the outer layer. Armadillos are small mammals with bony plates that slide over each other, so they can move easily. If a predator gets too close, the armadillo rolls up tightly into a hard, bony ball.

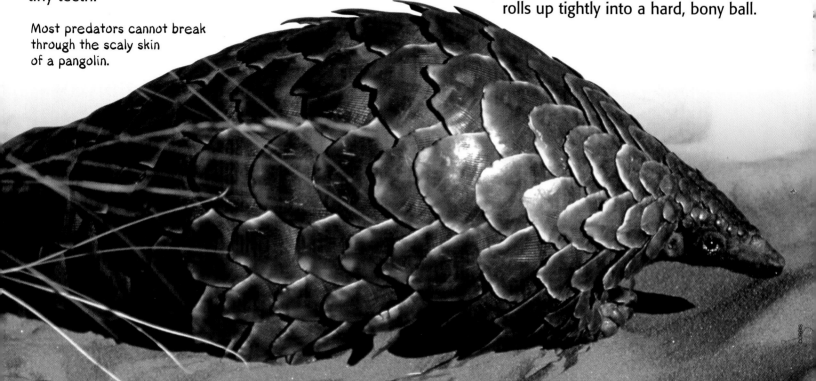

Animals

Wiggly snake

WHAT YOU NEED

beads

colored construction paper

paper fasteners

sequins

gluestick

tape

scissors

pipe cleaner

pencil

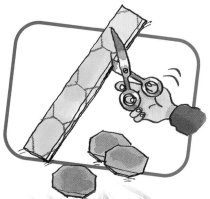

1 Cut some wide strips of construction paper. Fold them in half lengthwise and tape down one edge as shown.

2 Draw and cut out enough oval shapes to make a long snake.

3 Poke holes in each end of the ovals and use paper fasteners to join them together.

Make a scaly snake family

4 Make a triangular-shaped tail from construction paper and fasten it to one end of the snake's body.

5 Glue two beads onto the head for eyes. Make a tongue with the pipe cleaner and decorate the body with colored sequins.

Best nests

T he most important jobs in building a nest are finding the right materials and putting them together in the right way. A bird's nest can be a simple hollow in the ground, or a fantastic, woven, hanging structure. Male bowerbirds build a nest and decorate it with all the bright objects they can find – colorful flowers, berries, shells, foil, or plastic. They replace the materials as the colors fade.

Cup shapes

To make a cup-shaped nest, the bird sits in the middle of all the materials it has collected and turns around in circles, pushing outward until the shape is right. Hummingbirds make the smallest cup-shaped nests – they are only one and a half inches (4 cm) across!

Weavers

If a male weaver bird wants to impress a mate, his nest must be the best! Weavers tie complicated knots with their beaks and feet. A nest starts as a hanging ring. By looping, twisting, and knotting strips of leaves, the bird then weaves the ring into a round hollow nest. Sometimes, a long entrance tunnel is added to keep snakes out.

Animals

WHAT YOU NEED

wire mesh

eggs

needle

brush

paints

feathers

bowl

paper

hay or dried grass

Nest eggs

Make a fluffy bird to sit on your nest

1 Create a nest shape with the wire mesh.

2 Using feathers, hay, grass, and twisted strips of paper, weave in and out of the mesh to create the nest.

3 Use the needle to make a hole at each end of the eggs. Blow out the inside of the eggs into a bowl as shown. Paint speckles on the eggs and place them in the nest.

Warm and woolly

Many animals have thick, furry coats to keep them warm in winter. When the weather starts to get warm, many animals molt, or shed their coats. We use this unwanted **fur** or wool to make clothes for ourselves.

Sheep's fleece

The fur we use most comes from sheep. In warmer weather, farmers cut off, or shear, the sheep's heavy coats with electric clippers. The fleece is then sent to a factory. At the factory, the fleece, or raw wool, is cleaned and spun into thread, called yarn. There are two types of yarn: woolen and worsted. The fine threads, or fibers, of woolen yarn are messy. In worsted, the fibers are combed flat. Worsted yarn is used to make smooth cloth.

Soft and silky

An angora rabbit has very long fur. When loose fur is combed from its coat and mixed with wool, it makes a soft, fluffy yarn. We also get soft, fluffy, mohair wool from the long, silky coats of angora goats.

Costly cashmere

The softest, most luxurious wool of all is called cashmere, or pashmina. It comes from the downy undercoat of the Kashmir goat found in mountainous regions of Asia. During the molting season, the fur is combed out by hand. One cashmere sweater uses fur from four to five goats, and a long coat takes thirty to forty fleeces. No wonder cashmere clothes are so expensive!

Animals

Fluffy sheep

Glue a stick fence around your patchwork field

WHAT YOU NEED

variety of textured paper

cotton balls

gluestick

paints and brush

scissors   poster board

sticks

white paper

1 Glue cotton balls onto a piece of paper. Paint some black and some white. Cut out when dry.

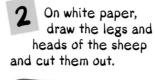

2 On white paper, draw the legs and heads of the sheep and cut them out.

3 Create a patchwork field by gluing squares of colored and textured paper onto your poster board.

4 Glue legs and heads onto the cotton balls. Now glue your sheep onto the patchwork field.

Sponge shapes

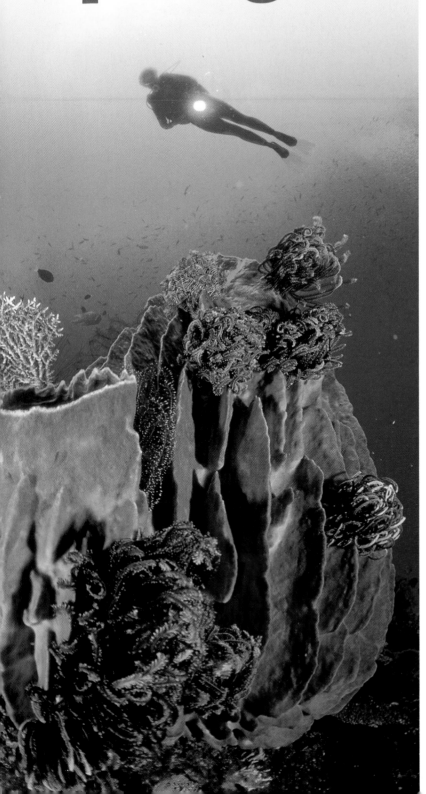

Did you know that the natural sponge you use in the bath is actually a living sea animal? Sponges live on rocks deep in the ocean. They are collected by deep-sea divers. Before they are sold, the living parts are removed and the sponge is cleaned, leaving the soft, spongy skeleton.

Strange sea animal

A sponge is not like any other living animal. A sponge does not even have a mouth! A sponge's body is filled with tiny holes, so water flows through it. Very tiny plants and animals in the water, called **plankton**, get trapped inside the sponge and are eaten.

Big and small

There are more than 5,000 different kinds of sponges. The biggest are seven feet (2 m), while the smallest are only about one inch (2 cm) long.

Useful sponges

People have used sponges for thousands of years. Greek and Roman soldiers padded their helmets and armor with them, and even drank from them. Today, we use sponges for cleaning things, as protective padding, and even for painting walls! Now we usually use **synthetic** sponges, so the natural sponges are left alone to grow in peace.

Animals

Sponge prints

Make colorful sponge pictures to hang on your bedroom wall

WHAT YOU NEED

white paper

paints

poster board

scissors

paintbrush

glue

sponge

toothpicks

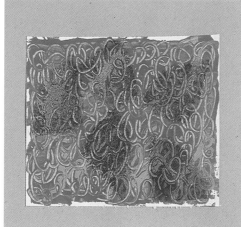

1 Mix colored paint with the glue.

2 Paint the mixture onto pieces of paper. Scratch patterns with a toothpick. Leave to dry.

3 Cut pieces of sponge into several shapes.

4 Paint the sponge shapes with different colors. Print them onto your textured surfaces. When dry, mount your pictures on poster board.

Spines and prickles

How do animals protect themselves from a hungry predator? One way is to have a spiky coat. If the animal cannot run very fast, it can stay still and use its spikes for **defense**. An animal covered in sharp spikes can protect itself from the fiercest predator.

Spiky back

The porcupine's back is covered in a double layer of long, black-and-white **quills**. When frightened, it rattles its quills to make them stand up and stamps its feet. If this does not scare away the predator, the porcupine rushes backwards at it. Sometimes, part of a quill is left in the other animal's skin.

Prickly ball

A **hedgehog's** coat of spikes only grows on the upper part of its body. The rest is covered in coarse hair. When a hedgehog is frightened, it rolls up. Its soft back part, head, and feet are tucked up safely into a prickly ball.

Spiky skins

The stickleback is a small fish that lives mainly in fresh water. When threatened, spikes on its back and tail lock upright. A predator gets a mouthful of spikes that are almost impossible to swallow. One family of sea animals is called **echinodermata**, which means "prickly skinned animals." It includes starfish and spiky sea urchins.

Animals

Spiky porcupine

WHAT YOU NEED

clay

beads or buttons

toothpicks

leafy stems

1 Roll the clay into a ball and form a snout at one end.

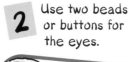

2 Use two beads or buttons for the eyes.

3 Stick the toothpicks into the clay all over the body.

4 Scratch on the nose and facial markings with a toothpick.

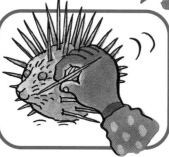

Make a leafy home for your porcupine!

19

Pouches and pockets

Marsupials are animals that have pockets, called **pouches,** in their skin. Kangaroos, koalas, and opossums are all marsupials. They use their pouches as safe places for their babies to grow. The koala's pouch is on its back, but kangaroos and opossums have pouches in front.

Safe inside

When a young marsupial is born, its eyes, ears, and back legs are not yet formed. Blind, deaf, and unable to walk for the first six or seven weeks, the baby needs to be protected from the outside world.

Joey

When a baby kangaroo, or **joey**, is born it crawls into its mother's pouch. This can take as long as five hours. Once inside, the joey finds one of its mother's four milk-giving teats and holds on by its mouth. It stays there for about eight months, only leaving the pouch when it is big enough to hop around.

Clinging koala

Koalas live in trees, so the female's pouch is on her back. The newborn koala crawls inside and stays there for seven months. When it comes out, the baby clings to its mother's back for another six to twelve months, until it is ready to set out on its own.

Animals

Drawstring bag

WHAT YOU NEED

scissors

material

needle and thread

yarn

safety pin

sequins

1 Cut a circle and a long, wide strip from your piece of material.

2 Sew the long strip together as shown.

3 Follow the picture to sew the circular piece of material to the long strip.

4 Create pockets by cutting out different pieces of material and then sewing them onto the sides of the bag.

5 Turn the bag inside out. Fold over the top edge of the bag and sew it down, leaving a gap.

6 To make the drawstrings, tie yarn onto a safety pin and push it into the gap. Thread the pin through the top seam of the bag. Draw out both ends and pull to close.

Sew or glue sequins onto the pockets, or use embroidery thread to decorate your bag.

Make a matching wallet or purse to go with your bag

21

Snapping jaws

If you want to find out what kind of food an animal eats, look at its teeth and jaws. They are specially made to suit its diet. Plant-eaters such as deer have broad, flat teeth for grinding up grass. Alligators, sharks, and other meat-eaters have razor-sharp teeth for tearing and ripping flesh. Animals that eat both plants and meat have both kinds of teeth.

Shark attack!

Sharks swim through the oceans, hunting for food without ever stopping. When they attack, their powerful jaws bite and their long, jagged teeth slice, killing **prey** in minutes. A shark's enormous jaws can open so wide it can swallow prey whole. It uses its razor-sharp teeth to tear off chunks of flesh. They grow in rows inside the mouth, and new teeth replace the old, worn-down teeth as often as once a week. Sharks usually hunt and eat other fish – it is rare that they attack people.

Alligator roll

Crocodiles and alligators have long, snapping jaws full of sharp, strong teeth. They live in shallow lakes, slowly moving rivers, and swamps. They stay out of sight below the water's surface, waiting for an animal such as an antelope or a deer to come close enough. They then rush at their victim, grab it in their powerful jaws, and drag it into the water. Holding it tightly, they kill their prey by rolling around with it under water until it drowns.

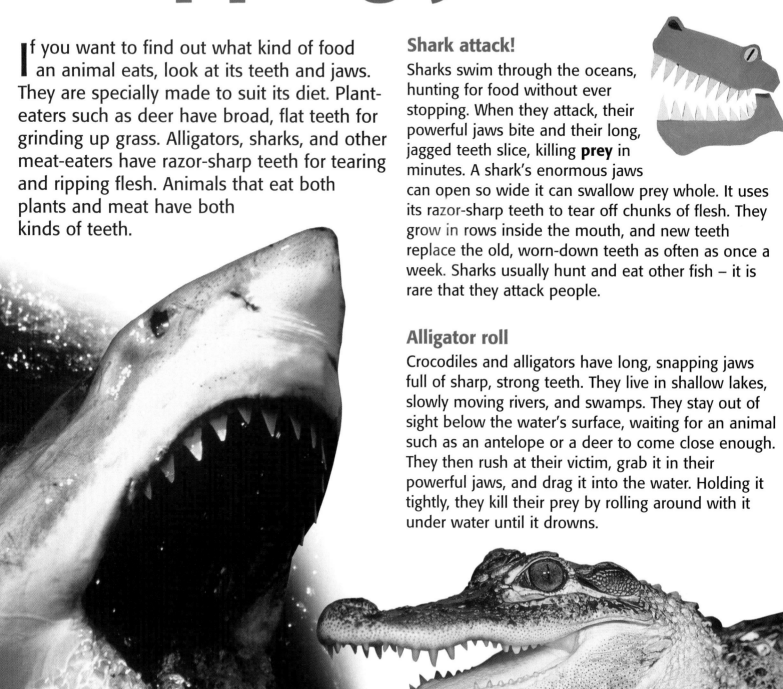

Animals

Alligator arm mask

WHAT YOU NEED

poster board and construction paper

pencil

scissors

paints

paintbrush

tape

1 Draw, in two parts, an outline of an alligator's head on the poster board. Cut it out carefully.

2 Paint each part of your mask green.

3 Use strips of construction paper to make rings to fit around your arms, and tape them to the back of each part of the alligator's head.

What other animals with snapping jaws can you make?

4 Place on each arm and make snapping movements.

23

Danger signals

If you see a small, brightly colored animal – beware! Many small animals use bright colors for protection. The colors warn hungry predators that the animals are probably **poisonous**. Other small animals have patterns on their bodies that are meant to warn, startle, or fool predators.

Warning wings

Birds are the main predators of butterflies and moths. The insects must frighten away the birds, or be eaten. A monarch butterfly's bright, warning colors are a signal to keep birds away. The butterfly's body contains chemicals that will make a bird sick if it is eaten. A harmless insect that mimics, or looks similar to another harmful insect, uses a defense called **mimicry**. The harmless viceroy butterfly is the same color as the poisonous monarch butterfly, so birds avoid it too.

Hidden stings

Bees and wasps have bright yellow and black-and-white bodies to warn predators to beware of their sting. The wasp beetle, found in Europe, looks exactly like a wasp, so enemies leave it alone as well. Beetles such as ladybugs also use their colors and patterns to defend themselves.

Poison frogs

Many frogs produce **poison** from glands in their skin, so they are not eaten. The poison-dart frogs that live in the rainforests of Central and South America produce some of the most powerful poisons ever found. Their jewel-like color and patterns send a clear message to predators – stay away!

Animals

WHAT YOU NEED

- two small plastic containers

- string
- poster board
- pipe cleaner
- paints and brush

- scissors
- sequins
- tissue paper
- glue
- silver and gold paints

1 Glue overlapping strips of tissue paper to the outside of the containers. Decorate with sequins and gold and silver paints.

2 Cut a slit in the top of each container. On poster board, draw and cut out two side panels for the containers and decorate.

3 Fold the straight edge and glue a panel to each container. Join the two containers together with a pipe cleaner. The pipe cleaner should fit over your nose.

Frighten your friends with horror headgear!

4 Make a spiked headband. Decorate and paint it.

5 Attach string to the headband and goggles. Tie the ends around your head. You are now wearing your fierce face mask!

You could also color the rest of your face with face paint.

Up and away

Perfect shape

Birds' wings are not all exactly the same shape. The woodpecker has short, rounded wings, so that it can turn quickly in forests with many trees. Pheasants have broad wings, so they can take off straight up into the air. The swift stays in the air for most of its life, flying at around 25 miles per hour (40 km/h). It only lands to mate and to lay eggs. Its slender, curved, pointed wings are ideal for non-stop flying. They lift the swift upward and are slim enough to cut through the air, keeping the bird from slowing down.

Super soarers

Most large birds soar and glide using the power of the wind to keep them up. Heavy **birds of prey** soar upwards on **thermals**. They ride on these columns of warm, rising air and only flap their wings to move from one thermal to another. A sea gull's long, pointed wings help it to glide on currents of air that bounce up from cliffs.

Hoverbird

To stay in one place in the air, a bird has to beat its wings continuously. Most birds can hover for only a short time. The bird that can hover for the longest is the kestrel. It beats its wings rapidly, but needs a slight wind to keep it up. The world's fastest flying bird is the peregrine falcon. It can dive to catch prey at an amazing 175 miles per hour (280 km/h)!

Have you ever watched a bird soaring through the air and wished that you could fly too? Birds' wings are shaped specially for flying. They are curved on top and slightly flatter underneath, so the air flowing over and under them lifts the bird into the air.

Animals

Swirly pictures

WHAT YOU NEED

paper

poster board

brushes

gluestick

feathers

glitter

paints

1 Using brushes and feathers, create a series of swooping strokes on your paper with paint.

2 Cut out your patterns and mount them on poster board.

3 Decorate some of them with glitter.

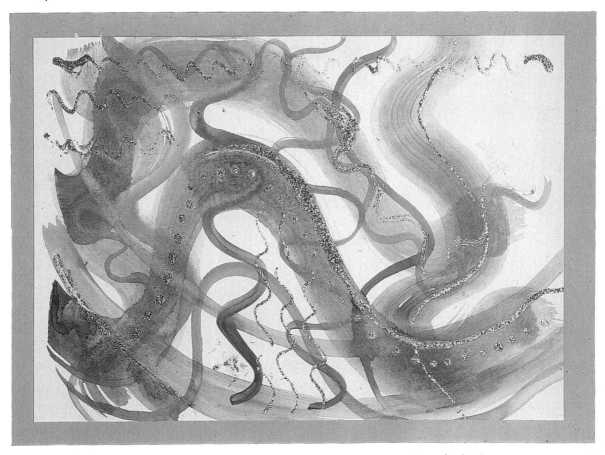

What else can you use to make unusual patterns and strokes?

Swing high!

Monkeys are real animal acrobats! They leap and swing through the treetops of their forest home. They balance, steer, and grip with their long, strong tails. Apes look very similar to monkeys, but are bigger, with longer arms, larger brains, and no tail. Apes and monkeys belong to the **primate** animal family, which also includes humans.

High life

Most monkeys spend their lives in the treetops. They find plenty of food there – fruit, nuts, and insects. Monkeys' bodies are ideal for living in and moving through the trees. They are slim and strong, with long arms, muscled legs, and long, curling fingers and toes. Monkeys have thumbs, so they can grip and hold things. They can even hang from a branch by their tails! When two monkeys rest together, they often hold tails to show they are friends.

Apes

Orangutans, gorillas, and chimpanzees are all apes. Apes are better climbers than monkeys, who prefer running and jumping. Apes also spend more time on the ground and walk more upright than monkeys. Like almost all primates, apes live together in close family groups.

Animals

Jungle monkeys

poster
board

paints and
brush

yarn or
string

colored pencils

scissors

pencil

1 Draw different monkeys onto the poster board, making sure the arms and tails curl, so the monkeys can hang from each other.

2 Cut them out and paint them different colors. When they are dry, use colored pencils to add detail.

Hang the monkeys from the leaves of a potted plant jungle

You can also make a monkey mobile. Attach string to one monkey and hang the rest from each other by their arms and tails.

29

Color-changer

A chameleon is an interesting animal. Its toes are joined together so that it can wrap its v-shaped feet tightly around branches. It has cone-shaped eyes that can swivel all the way around to spot its prey. As for changing color, a chameleon is the best!

Trickster

Most people think that a chameleon changes color to match its background, but its natural color is green or brown, so it already blends in with the forest. Its skin color makes it difficult to see and helps it to hide from predators. If a chameleon is seen, it has some tricks for escaping, such as flattening itself to look like part of a branch.

A chameleon can also puff itself up and open its mouth wide to hiss. If this doesn't work, it may drop off its branch onto the forest floor, where it will be hidden again.

Color-making cells

A chameleon's color changes as the light and temperature around it change. It also changes color when it is angry or scared. There are three layers of color cells in the chameleon's skin. The tiny, color-making parts inside the cells move to turn the chameleon different colors, even bright shades of yellow and red. Male chameleons often turn a bright color to attract a female.

Animals

Draw a scene with a lot of chameleons hidden in it

WHAT YOU NEED

colored construction paper

gluestick

pipe cleaners

tissue paper

scissors

sequins

pencil

sticks

straws

1 Draw an outline of a chameleon on a piece of green construction paper and cut it out – head, body, and legs.

2 Decorate your chameleon with small pieces of tissue paper rolled into balls, straws cut into small circles, and sequins.

3 Glue these onto your chameleon.

4 Use a pipe cleaner to outline the mouth.

5 Glue the chameleon on another piece of construction paper and glue the sticks underneath its feet.

6 Glue on a brightly colored pipe cleaner to make the chameleon's long, curly tongue.

31

Coral reefs

A **coral reef** is a beautiful sea garden. Many wonderful plants, animals, and fish live on and around it. The coral is built from the skeletons of tiny **coral polyps**. It forms fantastic shapes which can look like curly leaves, giant mushrooms, lacy fans, or tiny pipes.

A sea garden

The living polyps are like orange, yellow, purple, or green flowers. Colorful starfish and **sea anemones** also live on the coral reef. Strange-looking tropical fish swim along it, searching for prey. They include beautiful angel fish, striped spiny lionfish, and tiny sea horses.

Tiny tubes

Coral polyps, the animals who build the coral, are like little cylinders. They have a mouth at one end surrounded by tiny, waving **tentacles**. Polyps live tightly packed together in groups called **colonies**.

Animal builders

The coral polyp's skeleton grows outside its body. It forms when the polyp takes in small particles of a **mineral** called **calcium** from the seawater. The calcium changes inside the polyp's body and is squeezed out to form the coral. As each new polyp grows, the coral reef also gets bigger.

The dramatic colors of a coral reef.

Animals

WHAT YOU NEED

cardboard box

tissue paper

wire

sand

shells

peach pits

sponge

silver foil

tape

paintbrush

paints

sequins

glue

Coral box

Stick seashells to the outside of your coral box

1 Rip strips of different colored tissue paper. Glue in enough strips to cover the inside of the box.

2 Cut the sponges into coral shapes and decorate them with sequins and paint.

3 Twist strips of silver foil and tissue paper together. Glue to the roof of the box so they hang down to the floor.

4 Glue the sponges inside the box. Cover the base of the box with glue and sprinkle sand on top.

5 Paint the peach pits. Make fins from tissue paper, glue to each end of a pit and decorate with sequins.

6 Wrap wire around your fish.

Poke small holes in the top of the box, thread the wire through and tape the ends. Hang the fish at different heights.

Fins and flippers

All swimming animals have fins or flippers so they can balance and push themselves through the water. Fish have only fins and penguins have only flippers. But dolphins, whales, and seals have both. Sea turtles, ducks, and sea gulls use their webbed feet like flippers, to paddle and steer through the water.

Flip-flops

Dolphins, whales, and seals are sea animals with flippers in place of legs. The powerful tail fins of dolphins and whales move them forward through the water. All dolphins and some whales also have a fin on top of their body, which keeps them upright in the water. Seals belong to the animal family called **pinnipeds**, which means "fin-footed." A seal's four swimming "legs" are more like flippers than fins. Seals live on land as well as in the sea, but they move awkwardly on land. They shuffle from place to place, using their powerful stomach muscles and their flippers to help them along.

Underwater flyers

Penguins are birds with flippers instead of wings. They are excellent swimmers, flying through the water in the same way that birds fly through the air. They swim underwater at a speed of about eight miles per hour (13 km/h) and come up to breathe once a minute. Penguins are also expert divers, plunging as deep as 900 feet (274 m) below the sea's surface.

Fishy fins

Most fish have fins on top, underneath, and on either side of their bodies. These help them to balance and to steer. Strong tail fins propel the fish forward. Fast-swimming sharks have about eight large, triangular fins, including a powerful tail fin, a single back fin, and several side fins.

A colony of Northern fur seals.

Animals

Dolphin sculpture

WHAT YOU NEED

clay

stones

paints and brush

glitter

stick

PVA glue

1 Divide the clay into two balls and roll between your hands to soften it.

2 Create a dolphin shape with one ball of clay and a rock shape with the other.

3 Make a hole in the top of the rock with the stick. The hole needs to be deep enough for the stick to stand up in it.

4 Push the top of the stick into the belly of the dolphin. Remove it once a hole has been made. Leave to dry.

Varnish your sculpture with PVA glue mixed with water.

5 Paint the dolphin and rock. Add glitter to make them shimmer.

Stand the stick in the rock and place the dolphin on top of it. Scatter stones around the base.

Make other sea animal models such as sharks and seals

A pelican is recognizable by its bucket-like beak.

Beaks and bills

If you want to know what a bird eats, just look at its beak! Some birds have very strange-looking beaks, such as a pelican's bucket-like beak and a flamingo's hooked, curved bill. A bird's beak is designed so that it can catch, hold, and eat its food.

Beak pouches

A pelican has a small head with an enormous beak that it uses to scoop up fish. The long, pointed beak has a pouch underneath that stretches to hold fish. The pelican's beak is like a fishing net with a lid.

Super sieves

A flamingo's beak is designed to work like a sieve. The flamingo lowers it into the water, then moves the bottom bill up and down. The water is pumped out, but tiny animals and plants are trapped in a fringe inside the top bill.

Curved beaks

Birds that wade in shallow water dig into the soft mud for worms and crabs. The curlew uses its very long, curved beak to poke deep into the mud, further than other birds can reach. The avocet has a beak that curves up. It sweeps it from side to side under the water to catch its prey.

Animals

Floating duck

plastic
bottle

newspaper

paints
and
brush

toilet
paper
roll

tape

poster
board

glue

varnish

scissors

1

Cut a plastic bottle in half and stuff it with newspaper. Glue the toilet roll on top of the open end of the bottle to make the head and stuff it with newspaper.

2 Create wings by drawing shapes on poster board and cutting them out. Glue the wings onto each side of your duck.

Make a family of ducks for your bathroom

3 Cut a piece of poster board in the shape of a beak. Tape it to the front of the duck's head.

4 Cover the whole duck with glue and stick on strips of newspaper.

5 When dry, paint your duck.

Finally, give your duck a coat of varnish to make it waterproof!

Feathers

Just as we wear clothes to keep warm, a bird wears feathers. These grow out of its skin and have many uses. They keep the bird warm and dry, they allow it to fly, they protect it from bumps and bruises – and they help the bird to blend in with its surroundings, so it can hide from predators.

Clean feathers

Birds spend several hours a day combing, or **preening**, their feathers with their beaks and feet. Feathers need to be kept clean in order to work properly. A small bird, such as a wren, has about 5,000 feathers. Larger birds, such as owls, have more than 10,000 feathers. A very large bird, such as a swan or an eagle, has more than 20,000 feathers.

Wing tips and tail feathers

Flight feathers are attached to the bird's wings and tail. These are broad, flat, and stiff, so they can push through the air when flying. An owl's flight feathers have very soft, furry edges that hardly make a sound as they swish through the air, so it can swoop down silently on its prey. A kestrel shivers its wings instead of flapping them, so that it can hover in one place, like a helicopter. Most birds fan out their wing tips and tail feathers, which work like brakes, slowing them down as they land.

Feathery patterns

The patterns and colors on some feathers help birds to blend in with their surroundings. The white feathers of a snowy owl, for example, blend in with the icy landscape of its **Arctic** home. Owls that live in forests, such as the tawny owl, are speckled brown so they can hide among twigs and branches.

Brand-new plumage

Once or twice each year, a bird grows new feathers to replace the old, worn ones. The new feathers grow quickly from the skin as the unwanted ones molt, or fall out. For a few days, the bird looks messy, but soon it has a bright new set of feathers, or plumage, and is ready to fly again.

STEFAN WINSTRAND/ BRUCE COLEMAN COLLECTION

Animals

WHAT YOU NEED

feathers

beads

wire

black string

Feathery necklace

Make sure you only use bought or found feathers!

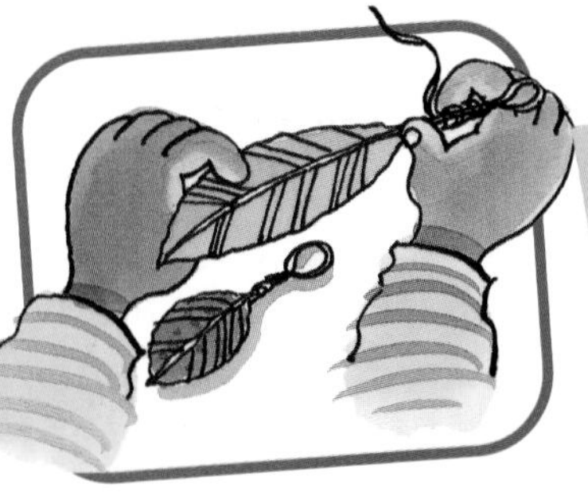

2 Thread the feathers onto a piece of string, with colored beads in between.

1 Select a variety of bright feathers. Make a loop with a small piece of wire and twist the ends around the quill of each feather.

All kinds of shells

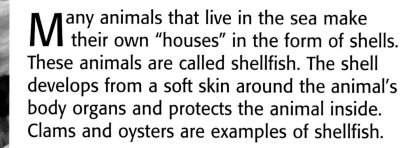

Many animals that live in the sea make their own "houses" in the form of shells. These animals are called shellfish. The shell develops from a soft skin around the animal's body organs and protects the animal inside. Clams and oysters are examples of shellfish.

Bivalves

A shellfish with two shells joined together by a hinge is called a bivalve. When the shells are open, water can be let in and out through two tubes. Bivalves come in different shapes and sizes. They include oysters, scallops, mussels, cockles, and clams.

Giant clam

The giant clam is the biggest bivalve of all. It can grow to 53 inches (135 cm) in length and live for hundreds of years. During the day, the clam opens to allow light in. Algae living inside the clam use the light to make food. The algae and clam depend on one another to live.

Body protection

Many animals without backbones, called **invertebrates**, grow shells. These are made of a hard substance called **chitin**. Some shells are part of the animal's body and grow with the animal. Other shells are rigid, which means that they do not grow and are shed, then replaced by a larger shell.

RANDY FARIS/ CORBIS

Animals

WHAT YOU NEED

filler paste

bowl

large stone

paintbrush

wooden spoon

shells and small stones

poster board

scissors

paints

Seashell paperweight

You can also decorate with beads, sequins, glitter, or colored stones

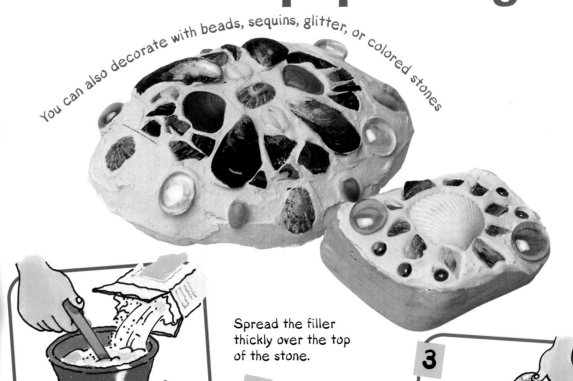

1 Mix the filler according to the instructions on the package.

Spread the filler thickly over the top of the stone.

2

3 Arrange the shells and stones by pressing them into the filler in a pattern.

4 When dry, paint the rest of your paperweight.

Make a picture frame

Use a piece of poster board to make the frame. You can cut the poster board into any shape you like. Then cut a rectangular hole in the middle, slightly smaller than the picture you wish to frame. Now follow steps 1 to 4 above to decorate your picture frame.

Light and dark

Many hunting animals have coats that are patterned or colored so that they blend in with their surroundings. This coloring is called camouflage. Camouflage helps an animal to stay hidden while **stalking** its prey. Leopards hide unseen in thorn trees, where their spotted coats blend in with the branches. Once they have made a kill, leopards often drag their prey back into the tree to eat.

Shadows in the dark

It can be dark on the floor of a rainforest, even during the day. Not much sunlight falls through the thick clusters of leaves and branches. In the gloom, a prowling animal may look just like a moving shadow. Some rainforest animals have such dark coats that at night only their eyes can be seen. The black panther's dark fur is covered with black spots, so that it easily blends into the forest at night.

White light

In the freezing Arctic, many animals have white fur which blends in with the snow around them. The large polar bear is difficult to see against the white landscape, so it can easily catch its prey. Every winter, the Arctic fox grows a coat of white fur, so it can stay hidden in the snow. When the snow melts in summer and uncovers the rough ground, the Arctic fox turns brown again and can still move around unseen.

Animals

Panther on the prowl...

WHAT YOU NEED

white pencil

black and white paper

scissors

gluestick

black tissue paper

2 Glue the panther shape onto a piece of white paper. Turn the paper over.

3 Tear strips of black tissue paper and glue them over the prowling panther, like a screen.

1 Draw an outline of a prowling panther on a piece of black paper and cut it out.

4 Hold your picture up to a light to see the shadow of the panther prowling through the jungle.

Add some jungle vines to your picture

You could stick your picture on the window

In disguise

D anger lurks deep in the rainforest! A hungry predator is waiting to pounce at every turn. The smaller rainforest animals must defend themselves in whatever way they can. Many of them use camouflage for protection. It helps them to blend in with the background, so they are hard to see. Some animals are even **disguised** as something else.

Toad leaves

Many animals rely on their natural skin patterns and coloring in order to blend in with their surroundings. An animal's skin coloring often reflects where it lives. Horned toads live on the rainforest floor. They are also called leaf litter toads. This is because their bodies are the same color as the dead leaves that have fallen to the ground. When a predator comes prowling, the toad defends itself by sitting very still among the leaves.

Invisible animals

Green tree frogs live in the trees, but it is very hard to see their bright-green bodies among the leaves. Other rainforest frogs can turn green, brown, or red to match their surroundings. Snakes, such as the tree boa, have **mottled** skin patterns that blend perfectly with their forest environment. A snake can also disguise its long, thin shape by coiling itself around the branches of trees. Green vine snakes, for example, look just like hanging vines.

In disguise

Some small animals are disguised as other animals or objects. Stick insects look exactly like twigs to fool hungry birds or foraging bush pigs. Leaf katydids look like grasshoppers and live in bushes and shrubs close to the ground. Their bodies are shaped like a crumpled leaf that has fallen from a tree. Few predators find dead leaves tasty, so the leaf katydids are safe. Other animals mimic, or pretend to be, animals that are dangerous or bad tasting. There is even a moth caterpillar that looks like a snake!

Animals

Secret jungle

WHAT YOU NEED

paints and brush

glue

tissue paper

scissors

small box

pencil

different shades of green construction paper

1 Draw a variety of leaves, trees, and plants on different pieces of green paper. Paint patterns on them and then cut them out.

2 Glue your leaves together to make different-sized plants and trees.

3 Cut out one side of the box and cover the rest with green tissue paper.

4 Draw and cut out several clumps of long grass shapes.

5 Fold up the bottom part of each plant cut-out to make a flap. Glue the flaps to the box, so the plants stand upright.

6 Draw and paint small animals, such as snakes and frogs, to hide in your jungle.

Can your friends spot the hidden animals?

Glossary

animal kingdom The category, or group, to which all animals belong.

Arctic The cold regions north of the Arctic Circle.

birds of prey Birds that hunt and kill other animals for food.

calcium A mineral that forms the basis of animal bone and shell.

camouflage The patterns or colors on an animal's skin that allow it to hide in its surroundings.

chitin A liquid substance which hardens to form an animal shell.

colonies Groups of the same type of animals or plants that live together.

coral polyps The individual animals in a colony of hard or soft corals.

coral reef The structure formed from billions of hard coral polyp skeletons.

defense Any form of protection against danger or attack.

dinosaurs Reptiles that first appeared about 230 million years ago. The word dinosaur means 'terrible lizard.'

disguise To change appearance in order to look like something else, or to hide.

display The use of colored body coverings to attract a mate or warn predators away.

echinodermata The family that includes starfish and sea urchins.

fur The coat of hair that some mammals have over their body.

hatchling Newly hatched animals.

hedgehog A small, insect-eating animal that is covered in spikes and lives in Europe.

herd A large group of mammals that live and feed together.

invertebrates Animals without backbones.

joey The name given to a baby kangaroo.

mammal A warm-blooded animal that produces milk for its young.

mating When two animals of the same species join together to make babies.

mimicry The use of colors and patterns by one animal to copy another animal's appearance.

mineral A general term for any of the major chemical ingredients that make up rock.

molt To shed, or get rid of, old skin, hair, or feathers.

mottled Marked with spots or blotches of different colors or shades of colors.

pinniped A member of the group of aquatic mammals that includes seals and walruses.

plankton Tiny sea plants and animals that live in waters closest to the water's surface.

plumage The feathers covering a bird.

poison Any substance that can cause damage or injury to the body, or even kill.

poisonous Capable of causing injury.

pouch A pocket of skin used to carry and hold baby animals.

predators Animals that hunt and kill other animals for food.

preening To smooth or clean feathers with a beak.

prey Animals that are hunted and eaten by other animals.

primate A member of the group of animals that includes apes, monkeys, and humans.

quills The stiff hollow spines of a porcupine or hedgehog and the large stiff wing or tail feathers of a bird.

rainforest Forested areas found in tropical regions near the equator.

reptile A cold-blooded animal that has scales and lays eggs on land.

scutes Bony scales that form the overlapping body armor of some fish and reptiles.

sea anemones Sea animals with tube-shaped bodies and tentacles around their mouthparts.

skeleton Framework of bone that supports the body.

stalking Creeping up quietly on prey.

synthetic A material that was made by people rather than found in nature.

tentacles Projecting parts of many animals, such as a jellyfish or an octopus, that can sense movement or heat.

Index

Materials guide

A list of materials, how to use them, and suitable alternatives

The crafts in this book require the use of materials and products that are easily purchased in craft stores. If you cannot locate some materials, you can substitute other materials with those we have listed here, or use your imagination to make the craft with what you have on hand.

Gold foil: can be found in craft stores. It is very delicate and sometimes tears.

Silver foil: can be found in craft stores. It is very delicate, soft and sometimes tears. For some crafts, tin or aluminum foil can be substituted. Aluminum foil is a less delicate material and makes a harder finished craft.

PVA glue: commonly called polyvinyl acetate. It is a modeling glue that creates a type of varnish when mixed with water. It is also used as a strong glue. In some crafts, other strong glues can be substituted, and used as an adhesive, but not as a varnish.

Filler paste: sometimes called plaster of Paris. It is a paste that hardens when it dries. It can be purchased at craft and hardware stores.

Paste: a paste of 1/2 cup flour, one tablespoon of salt and one cup of warm water can be made to paste strips of newspaper as in a papier mâché craft. Alternatively, wallpaper paste can be purchased and mixed as per directions on the package.

Cellophane: a clear or colored plastic material. Acetate can also be used in crafts that call for this material. Acetate is a clear, or colored, thin plastic that can be found in craft stores.

WHAT YOU NEED

gold foil

silver foil

filler paste

PVA glue

flour

salt

cellophane or acetate

1 2 3 4 5 6 7 8 9 0   Printed in the USA 0 9 8 7 6 5 4 3 2